Getting Along:
THE ABC's OF HUMAN RELATIONS

Getting Along:

THE ABC's OF HUMAN RELATIONS

Cartoons by ALLAN HIRSH Text by DONNA SINCLAIR

Wood Lake Books Winfield BC, Canada

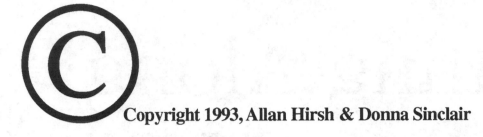

Copyright 1993, Allan Hirsh & Donna Sinclair

Published by
Wood Lake Books Inc.,
Box 700, Winfield, BC
Canada V0H 2C0

Printed in Canada by
Hignell Printing Ltd.,
Winnipeg, MB R3G 2B4

Editing and page design: Jim Taylor
Cover: Lois Huey Heck and Allan Hirsh

Canadian Cataloging in Publication Data

Sinclair, Donna, 1943–
   Getting Along

ISBN 0-929032-80-2

1. Interpersonal relations. 2. Social
 interaction.   I. Hirsh, Allan, 1948–
II. Title
HM1 32.S55   158'.2   C93-091868-1

Foreword

by **Lynn Johnston**

We argued, we threatened, we cried… Finally we ended up as a family on the doorstep of one Allan Hirsh, family counsellor.

Like countless others, we were the distressed parents of a teenaged son "with an attitude." (He, on the other hand, was saddled with us.) The itch-scratch-itch cycle firmly established, we were pilgrims desperately seeking relief.

Auuugghhhhh!

The "therapist's office," sparsely furnished with a rigid no-nod chair, an appropriately cluttered desk, and a nondescript but inviting looking couch, had instant appeal. There were toys. Lots of them. Dinky Toys, most of them, lined up on shelves next to boxes of Kleenex and reading materials with titles like *Zen through Bowel Sounds.*

My husband and I smiled at each other and said to ourselves, "Anyone who likes toys is okay in our books."

And so we allowed Allan Hirsh to turn a few pages of our lives.

It was an interesting adventure, opening up our lives to someone for analysis.

Our son Aaron, the catalyst for this process, wasn't as cooperative. He stalled, he complained, he missed appointments—and then one day he met the therapist on neutral ground. Familiar territory. The comic-book store. A private connection was made on the spot. And more pages were turned.

It was not so much the unravelling of the knotted interpersonal fabric of our family or the unburdening of lifetime loads that made these visits so valuable—it was the laughter we shared with the man who made us aware of how our family puzzle pieces fitted together. Allan Hirsh is blessed with the healing gift of humor, and the ability to transfer his wit from insight to comic illustration. This is truly neat! And truly rare.

I am an employed cartoonist (also very rare). When I first saw Allan's cartoons, I knew that behind the nodding and appropriately concerned countenance there was more than a therapist at work—there was a soulmate.

Many people try to draw funny pictures. Few possess the loose genetic screws that make this magic possible. Despite the simplicity of his drawing style, Allan's talent is richly evident and very unique.

During the past four years, our family has matured. Our son has left home to seek his fortune (broke, but happily working for a TV studio in B.C.). And our relationship with Allan Hirsh has become a close personal one. I look forward to Friday afternoons, when my friend the therapist/cartoonist arrives with another bundle of linear wit for my perusal and commentary. I generally arrange his offering in four piles: Great, Good, Needs work, and Hunh? But despite his deferrent mumblings of gratitude, we are equals.

Now, fortunately, Allan Hirsh, cartoonist/therapist, has collaborated with Donna Sinclair, writer of sensitive prose, to produce a meaningful, positive, and humorous look at relationships. And do these two know relationships! Their book is an easy read that finds you looking forward to the next page, much as you look forward to the next deep breath on a fresh spring day.

It is my great pleasure to be writing these notes for a book my friend Allan Hirsh has illustrated. And I hope it does well, because... well, because a good therapist should have toys in his office. Lots of them.

cknowledgments

In a way, everyone either Allan or I know needs to be thanked for their contributions to this book. It has grown, after all, out of many years of observing the way people (including each of us) interact with each other. Listing all those people by name might have a salutary effect on sales. It would, however, take a lot of space.

But there are some people without whom this book wouldn't have been written. Allan would especially like to thank Lynn Johnston, creator of the "For Better or For Worse" comic strip,for her support, guidance, and friendship. He calls her his "cartooning counsellor." He'd also like to thank his parents, for teaching him how important it is to have humor in the house.

I'd like to thank Jim Sinclair for almost thirty years of surprising me into laughter, and our children, for watching hawk-like, and commenting, on the ways I relate to other people. Including them. Especially them.

And both of us would like to thank our Jung group. They already know everything we've tried to put down here, and then some.

Introduction

This book grew out of a friendship and a conviction. Allan Hirsh and I have been members, for many years, of a small group devoted to the idea of discussing the ideas of Carl Jung. I say "the idea of discussing" literally. Sometimes we discuss Jung, sometimes dreams, but mostly we leave all that aside and focus on matters of survival in the field of relationships.

All this time Allan was doing cartoons, which he brought to our Jung meetings. As his small characters began to illuminate questions we were discussing, the notion of a book that would share these small, *angst*-filled, pot-bellied creatures with the world began to grow.

What people need, we decided, is a small guide to human relationships, a map through the flawed and sometimes risky terrain of love and/or marriage and/or parenting.

People need to have ways of talking to one another about how they are feeling.

So we decided on an ABC to help people—mainly at midlife, although anyone is welcome—who are trying to become literate in the horrifically complex language of intimate human interaction. Most of our readers will know the small characters on these pages in their bones; they are all of us. It's just that most of us need a verbal language to describe what they are about, and a visual language to see their situation.

Here are some words and phrases in that language. You can use them to tell the important people in your life what is going on in your heart and mind. We hope they will be useful.

A word of caution, though. This isn't a standard reference book. That is, while you may get something useful out of simply looking up the letter D, or M, or V, you'll get a lot more out of those letters if you read what comes before them first. In developing this open book, we've tried to open you up, as you open up the pages. You are more than random facts; because you open up progressively, step by step, that's the way we've written this book, too.

—Donna Sinclair

nalysis

You might think analysis only goes on in the therapist's office. It doesn't. A constant attempt to bring to consciousness the hidden factors that govern the way we are—our fears, our lack of self-esteem, our childhood wounds—takes place in all of us.

Especially after midlife. It's no accident that long suppressed memories of childhood abuse, for example, often surface only after 40. That's when we are strong enough to take it. That's when many of us have done enough work in the world, developing our outer selves, to have the confidence to begin examining our inner selves.

Self analysis is good work, worthwhile. If we don't do it, our unresolved pasts may rise up and demand more and more attention; we may have powerful nightmares that attempt to break through to the surface of our daily lives. Or we may become depressed, restless, dissatisfied. We may consider changing partners, jobs, locations, lives. The restlessness is healthy, but you may avoid inflicting needless pain on yourself and others if you take some time to figure out what makes you tick. A sabbatical from all volunteer work, perhaps, or from everything except what is needed to pay the rent. Take the time to record dreams. They will offer clues to what is unfinished inside you. Read books, talk to someone who matters to you about your inner workings, do some analysis of the side of yourself you don't know.

It's time. Be our guest—use this book to help you.

Abandonment

Unknown territory is scary for all of us, even at midlife. Most of us have a terrible fear that we will be lonely; perhaps the fear is left over from our childhood, when we feared above all else abandonment by our parents, protectors, guardian angels. The unknown territory of our own selves is as scary as any other jungle.

Best to take a friend with you. That means a good friend, someone you can trust to listen to the wonderings of your heart without sharing them with the world.

Sometimes, if you are lucky, you can find groups that are brave enough to do this: some spiritual study groups, some creative writing groups (dealing with your own poetry is a voyage inwards), some dream groups. If you can find enough like-minded people, one or two or four, you can study the reflections of **anyone** who is wise, and discover you are talking about yourself. Jung will do. So will Jeremiah.

Aerobics

Coming to understand yourself more fully may lead you into unexpected areas. I have a friend who suddenly, in midlife, started a fitness program, lost forty pounds and became an aerobics instructor. Until then, her life had been primarily academia: books, music, art, things of the mind...

What happened was a midlife surge of interest in the life she had not yet led. She had the courage to follow it (without, of course, giving up her interest in art and literature, or her job).

The key is to find what has been banished from your life that you need and seek it. For some it is a physical life. For many, in this too-rational age, it may be spirituality, faith, passion, and art.

Assertiveness

You may find yourself changing in surprising ways as you embark on an inner study. As you begin to live out some of what has been hidden inside, you may discover you have more energy. That's because until now it has taken immense effort to contain your own unused self and keep it from your own awareness. As that self is released, energy becomes available for other, more valuable tasks.

Sometimes that energy may come out as anger which is not the same as assertiveness—at the raw deal you've been living with all this time, or perhaps the raw deal you gave yourself.

You also may find yourself empowered. Men may find themselves with the energy and courage to be intimate and vulnerable to one another. And women, especially, may find themselves freed from cultural norms that suggest they should always be ladylike and soft.

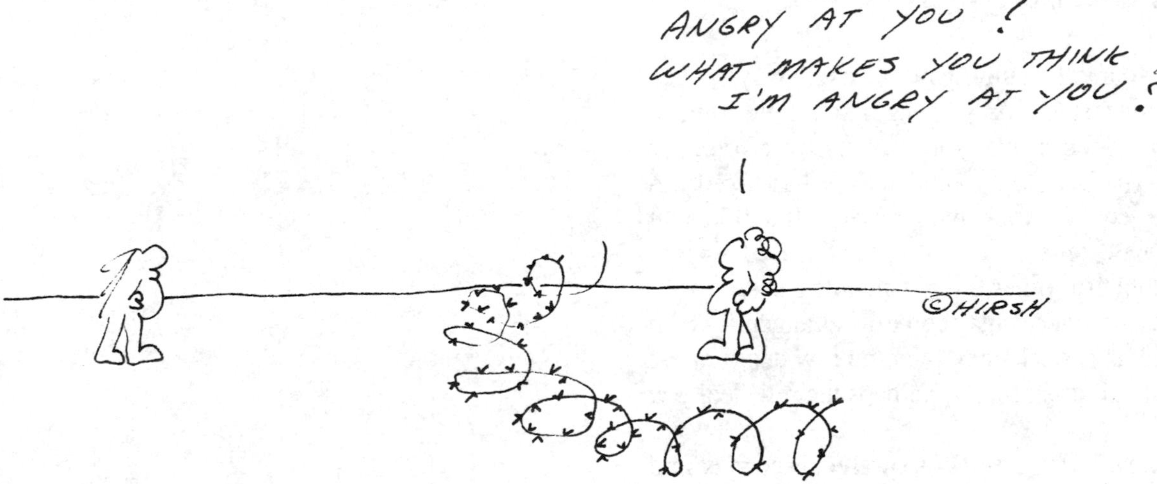
ANGRY AT YOU ?
WHAT MAKES YOU THINK
I'M ANGRY AT YOU ?
©HIRSH

Barbed wire

Not a good thing to have, even metaphorically, between people. Especially not people you love. See Barriers on the next page.

B oundaries and barriers

Relationships often founder over our inability to understand the difference between these two terms.

It's good to have psychic boundaries, to know where you and your responsibilities begin and end. It's good to know what your values are, what you believe, in whom you believe, and—as one friend of mine with wide experience in justice issues puts it—what you are "willing to go to the wall for." It's good to have a clear sense of self, and to know where you will not be compromised. That is part of what this book is about.

It's also good, paradoxically, to avoid creating insurmountable barriers between you and others. To be whole we need to be able to be vulnerable to others, unafraid to entertain notions that are diametrically opposed to those we usually hold. You can do that more easily if you know who you are, if you have examined what you believe, and have **said** it out loud.

It's also good to be open to another's feelings, able to sit—not walk away—while someone cries or is angry, even at you. (Not abusive. There's a crucial difference between anger and abuse.) It's good to be able to say what you mean, and to let your own feelings and affections and angers show.

None of this is easy, especially if the field of human relationships into which you have wandered has been more a minefield than a place to pick flowers. But understanding when to be open, when to risk trust, when to allow someone else access to your heart may make the difference between loneliness and intimacy. (We could also have put all this under A for authenticity, or T for transparency; the point seemed to belong best here.)

Burnout

Burnout has many causes. Everyone knows what happens when a high-achiever type meets insurmountable stress and neglects self-care, especially exercise. What is less well-known is the way intimacy, honesty, and authenticity in relationships helps people avoid burnout.

Not that burnout is an entirely bad thing. If it forces us to the therapist's office and encourages us to make friends with ourselves, then it is a good thing. One Jungian analyst says that everyone comes to analysis on their knees. Given the cost of professional therapy sessions, that's probably because we have been dragged there over the audible protests of our chequebooks.

Still, it's probably easier to talk our way through things with a good friend, one who is capable of dealing with our inner as well as outer world, before we collapse.

How shall we find such friends? With a good dose of intuition, a healthy sense of your own boundaries (and willingness to state them), but also with some practice in dismantling barriers and being vulnerable. The right person may already be there, but you've kept him or her away with your own barriers. It's always worthwhile keeping a careful eye open for groups of people who can handle intimacy.

Communication 1

Most of the millions of words written about communication in relationships can be summed up in a few aphorisms.

1. Share your feelings

Relationships founder when people don't tell each other how they feel. Unfortunately, many people are so out of touch with their feelings they don't know what they **do** feel.

One way to find out is to watch for dreams with a feeling tone to them—they'll sometimes give you a clue. And listen to whatever you find yourself humming during the day. Once, feeling burdened by a general lack of privacy, I found myself singing Bonnie Raitt's "Let's give them something to talk about" non-stop. Then I clued in. But I hadn't been able to take steps to get more privacy until I realized how mad I was about not having it.

Once you have deciphered what you feel—anger, affection, fear—work on why. Does this feeling belong to some inner juices of your own, or are they the result of an action by the other person? Is it, in other words, an appropriate feeling? A mate's failure to put the top back on the toothpaste, for example, is probably not cause to end a marriage. It might be wise to check out why you have a neatness neurosis. On the other hand, the drip drip drip of constant criticism may be an appropriate cause for feeling anger or despair.

You can explain your feelings by saying "I feel (fill in feeling) when you (fill in action)." That's more likely to be successful in developing the relationship (although perhaps not as satisfying) than "You jerk! You always... etc."

Communication 2

2. Accommodate occasionally

The ability to give a little (even when you know you are right) is a useful tool in relationships. As long as it isn't overused. And as long as it isn't always the same partner who accommodates.

Some matters can never be resolved. In that case, you can choose, if you wish, to live with that permanent disagreement. The main thing is to know what you are willing to accommodate, and what is not negotiable. Most of us, for example, can cope (as my spouse has) with someone (me) who will never learn to put the top back on the peanut butter. He accommodates. He even puts the top back on, patiently, day in and day out, for the sake of not having it ooze all over the cupboard if it tips over. For this, I love him. (And for other reasons too—but that generosity of spirit is certainly one of them.)

Of course, it's unwise for anyone to accommodate to being demeaned or humiliated, and certainly not to being physically assaulted. Get support and—if necessary—get out.

Communication 3

3. Listen

When someone tells you how they feel, look them in the eye. Don't talk. Don't say "But I..." Wait until they finish. Then say "You feel _____" (and fill in the blank.) Make sure they **feel** heard.

Don't defend yourself—especially if you're the cause of their feelings. Don't give reasons. Just listen.

This may solve the problem right away, without even doing anything more. You might feel you are able to say "I'm sorry. I didn't know you felt like that." Try to be open to being enlightened.

On the other hand, you are now entitled to a bit of time to tell your side. If you have modeled well the idea of listening (and if you have made a contract at the beginning to listen to each other without interrupting) your partner/friend/spouse/child may now be able to listen to you in the same manner. She/he may now be able to say to you. "I hear you saying that you feel_____ because _____."

This might be a good time to stop and let everything digest for awhile.

Never try to tell anyone how they **should** feel. Feelings don't have "shoulds" attached to them. They just are. Actions have shoulds. We shouldn't hit each other, be cruel to each other, denigrate one another. But our feelings are our own, and are to be respected.

Communication 4

4. Respect Differences

One of the difficulties of living in relationship with someone (anyone!) is that no two people are ever alike. That's also one of the pleasures; but at times of stress, we are tempted to re-shape the other in our own image. This doesn't work.

Better to try to objectify your differences, make them something "out there," separate from the two of you and your relationship, a given which can be equably discussed, like the weather. Then you can figure out ways to get around it, just the way you wear a raincoat when it rains, instead of trying to change the rain to sunshine.

With personality testing, you may discover—for example—that one of you is an introvert and one an extrovert. In our family, I'm the introvert, my spouse the extrovert. He is energized by people, loves parties, talks about what he thinks, and comments on everything we encounter as we go for walks.

I like to be quiet. At parties, I find one person and talk to him or her all evening. And I think about what I'm going to say for so long that conversation generally has gone on to something else before I can open my mouth. However, what I have thought through is so solid to me that I sometimes think I've said it anyway.

You can imagine how this combination works. Misunderstandings abound. And there are other combinations of personalities too. Some types wander through life knowing what to do in any circumstance because "it feels like the right thing;" others think their way through carefully, and can only really understand another's feeling when the "feeler" can describe it in very clear and logical words.

But each person's patterns are caused, not by stubborn-

ness or senility or cantankerousness, but by the way we are made. Differing personality types are not an excuse for friction, but they are a reason.

So, about the introversion/extroversion: we agree that on walks he will try not to make the same comment about the same house we always pass, telling me the same story about its occupants that I have heard several times. And I agree to let him know, once in awhile, what I am thinking and feeling. The peculiar noises of despair he makes when he thinks of a story he would like to tell just one more time make me laugh.

And I have learned, when we entertain, what a gift it is to have someone there who will move the conversation along, and tell funny stories. Most of all, it's wonderful to be married to someone who knows how to penetrate the awful silence that introverts can create when they are not in a good mood.

Furthermore, since we are both "intuitive feelers" we both make judgements by instinct, and value the same things, often incomprehensible to most of the rest of the world. Mutual validation (See V) is a wonderful thing.

(For more on personality types, see—guess what—Personality Types, under "P.")

Communication 5

5. Stay in the present

Raise what is bothering you quickly, and—as much as possible—deal with the present, not the past. This is harder for some of us than others. If we have a lot of difficulty getting in touch with our feelings, it may take a couple of days before we even notice we are angry.

But if you don't deal with issues in relationship, and talk them out, they will spill out on their own. They have their own irreconcilable energy, and they will demand to be heard somehow. You will kick the dog or accidentally break someone's favourite mug, or pick a terrible fight in public. Don't wait until your feelings erupt like a runaway volcano and provide free entertainment to the masses. Talk about it now.

Communication 6

6. Don't triangulate

Most of us find it so intimidating to express anger or hurt that we will talk to almost anyone else before we will make ourselves vulnerable to the object of that emotion.

Most of us choose to mutter away to another member of the family, so that our annoyance has a chance to be made known, but only indirectly. Indirect is the operative word here. "Your father never ...; Well, you know, your sister has this habit of..." This creates an interesting triangle: you, the person you are annoyed with, and an innocent go-between who would rather not be there.

Triangulation also accomplishes very little. Painful though it may be at the time, it's better in the long run to be direct and talk it out with the person involved.

Communication 7

7. Cherish one another

Even when you are angry. Especially when you're angry.

Children 1

1. Bonding

Children will grow up some day. Until then, let them be children.

Children are people too. They deserve some healthy neglect. Contrary to what some parents believe, children do not need adults breathing down their neck all the time. They need space to daydream, to make some choices (even wrong ones), to fail or triumph. Don't take it all away from them.

hildren 2

2. Choice

Children need to learn to make choices. When they are little they can choose their clothes in the morning and what they will have for lunch and how they will spend their allowance. If money is tight, give them a very small allowance. But let *them* choose how they will use it. Or perhaps, how they will waste it. It's their choice.

Making choices for them—because as an adult you know better—is bad training. When they reach adolescence they will have to make a lot of tough choices on their own. You won't be there. Let them learn what the consequences of their choices are before the consequences get so large as to be life-threatening.

Children 3

3. Conflict

Children learn far more from what we **do** than from what we **say**. (How many of your ways of dealing with life were deliberately taught to you? And how many were just picked up from your parents and from people around you?)

If you want your children to enjoy good relationships when they are older, use all the tools for conflict resolution (see Communication, earlier in this book) while they are with you. They will learn.

They will learn from everything, good and bad, that you do.

hildren 4

4. Don't panic

The times when you're having the most difficult time with your children may be the times when they are most valuable to your own development. Children put you in touch with your own inner child; they can heal areas of yourself you didn't know were wounded. They can offer you a wonderful model for living joyously.

As a friend once commented: "We have children to help us grow up."

(Want more? Try Teenagers under T.)

ontrol

There are a lot of books about "taking control" of our lives, and most of us struggle nobly to do that.

But there is also an argument to be made for not being in control. A friend of mine shares with me her "canoe dreams." I have them too, dreams in which I am paddling a canoe, or find someone I love under a canoe in the water.

The canoe is a good symbol to describe a healthy attitude towards control. You do have to control the craft; it is self-propelled. No-one is providing a motor for it. It's all your own muscle that makes it go. But put a canoe on a windy lake or a rushing river, and you understand how important it is to work **with** the elements, not to try to control them.

That's how relationships work, too. Nothing wrecks a relationship faster than the sense that one partner is always in control, always in charge, never able to bend. When we are on the receiving end of that, we are driven right back into childhood and the identity struggle that never entirely ceases to haunt us.

enial

One of the most amazing things humans do to themselves is to hide from reality by pretending it doesn't exist. Many of us refuse to allow ourselves legitimate feelings—especially anger or grief—even when those feelings are entirely appropriate.

We may watch a relationship crumble, insisting that everything is all right when we really need counselling. We may insist we are well when we are really encountering chest pains or mysterious lumps. We may watch our children facing real problems, telling ourselves at the same time that this will pass.

Dreams have a way of circumventing denial. We may declare endlessly that nothing bad is happening to us in daily life; but at night, if we watch our dreams, we will be told the truth in symbolic form.

Even then it is tempting to deny. Members of a caring dream group can be very helpful if they will raise—slowly and carefully—the issues they see in your dreams.

Denial is not, in itself, a bad thing. Sometimes we can get through a short-term crisis by refusing to acknowledge it for awhile. But eventually, we have to stop and breathe and deal with it. That often happens at midlife, when we may confront a lot of issues we may have been denying most of our lives.

epression

Being depressed can be an opportunity. I know. But who wants to hear that Pollyanna statement from the middle of a black hole?

Depression may be situational. In fact, depression may be the most appropriate response to a whole lot of awful things, such as overwhelming grief.

Or depression may be the result of a massive quirk of body chemistry. If so, you should consult a physician.

Or it may be anger turned inward. If it is that last, depression offers you a chance to get in touch with its causes, name them, and begin some healing. Unless you are very strong, you will need help with this.

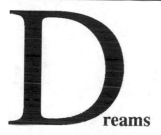

Dreams

You will have noted, if you have read any other parts of this book, frequent references to dreams. That's because they are an important way to the kind of self-understanding that enriches relationships with others. They're not the only way; some of us have great trouble remembering dreams, and even more trouble hearing what they might be saying. But they can be a powerful comment on how we are getting along with people.

You can capture those comments by simply writing as much as you can remember of your dreams in the morning in a notebook. Then you simply look at all the people and objects in the dream. And very gently—because this is holy ground and all these creatures and people, all this landscape is your soul—you ask what part of you this is. Perhaps a runaway car in a dream suggests your life is out of control.

Perhaps an old house filled with rare antiques points out how you are filled with unnamed treasures, and need to gather your self-esteem around you.

This isn't easy. All of us dream of thieves and tramps, whores and robbers, as well as gentle children and loving grandparents and guardian animals. But all these inner creatures should be treated with respect; this is the area of myth, your own myth. You don't want to hurt it. Nor to reject it.

Besides, when you face a monster within, you may discover it was only trying to get your attention. When it does, it may be transformed—as in Beauty and the Beast—into something beautiful.

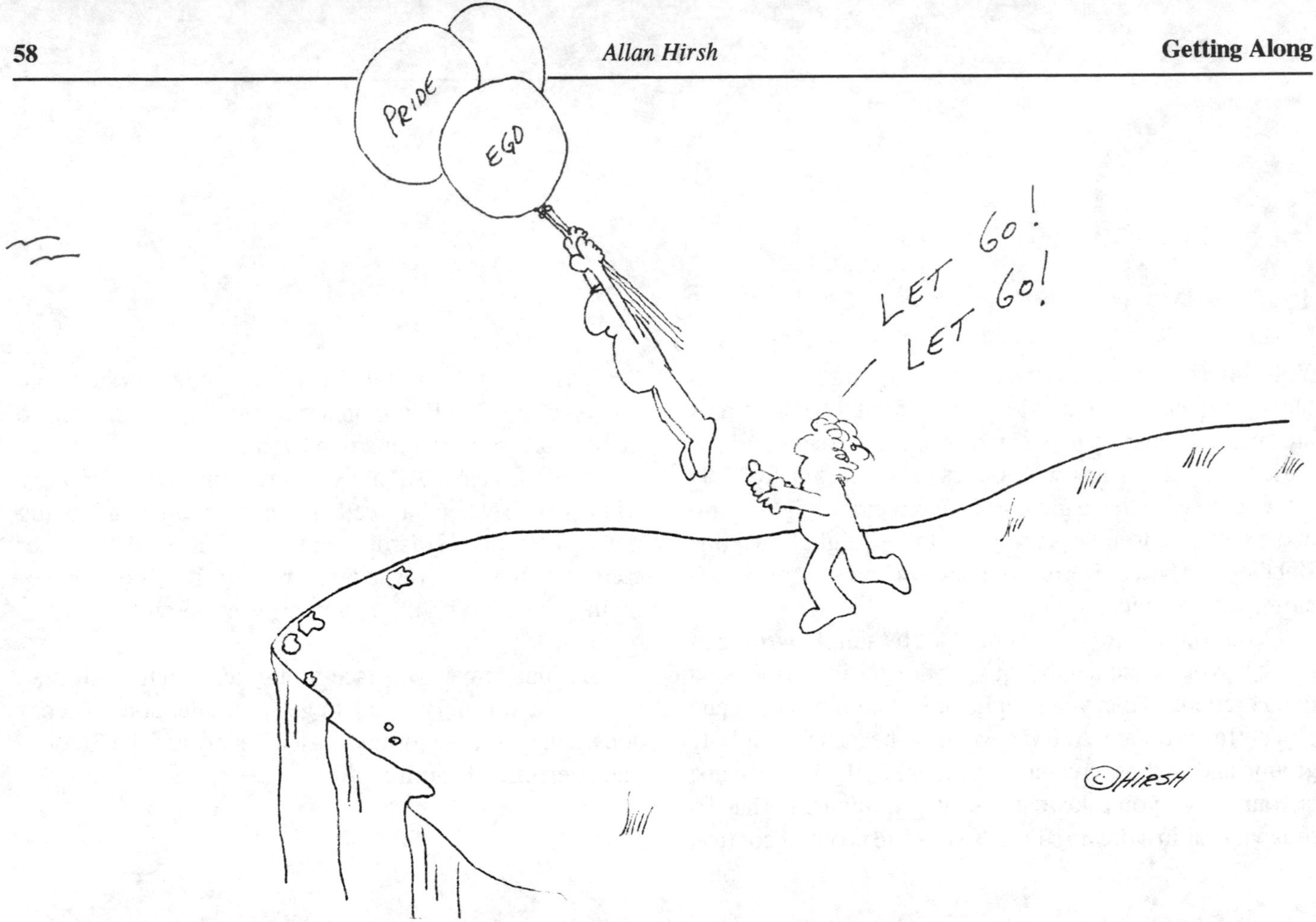
PRIDE
EGO
LET GO!
LET GO!
©HIRSH

E go

Think of driving a car, checking your rearview mirror, glancing sideways occasionally. We all know it's important to pay attention to things that are just out of the line of sight. If we don't, we could get blindsided.

The term "ego" is about what is already in your line of sight, pschologically speaking. It's the term for your conscious self, the self of which you are aware. There is a lot more to us, of course; but it is hard for the ego to understand that. It thinks it is all there is. And we are inclined to go along with that, because by definition the **un**conscious part of us is **un**known. But it is there, affecting us like mad.

Too strong a reliance on our rational side, on what we perceive to be our own intellect and logic as a way to guide us through life, is like driving a car without ever looking behind or to the side. It's like taking off in a hot air balloon without knowing about air currents. We can crash if we don't pay attention to what we can't see.

Further, it is a dangerous form of pride to think we can go it alone, straight ahead, without paying attention to our inner self. Better to let go of the ego if it is out of control, and trust other parts of ourselves—like intuition—as well.

Egocentric

It's perfectly normal to be the centre of your own universe. It is perfectly healthy to be responsible for your own life, and not to expect that someone else will offer you happiness or wealth. Relationships become unhealthy when one partner dissolves him or herself in the other; always accommodates, always gives in, always believes the other is the wise one, always believes the other will provide. So a little egocentricity is a good thing.

However, a little egocentricity can go a long way. A lot of it can go much too far. Part of being mature is the ability to see oneself as part of a larger whole, a community in which all are equally loved by God.

The way you understand this may depend on your cultural background and even on your sex. Within the Judeo-Christian tradition, much—perhaps too much—energy has been invested on notions of unworthiness and humility, to a point where it has encouraged passivity and an acceptance of hierarchy, an acceptance that others have authority over you. Women especially have been encouraged to be meek.

Best to see egocentricity as a relative term. If you don't have enough, a little seasoning of it won't hurt.

Family of origin

The kind of family we grow up in is where we learn about everything that's important: money, sex, God, how to fight, and how to love. We can spend all our lives in therapy, and the influence of that family of origin will never quite leave us. There will always be a ghost—mother saying this, father saying that—somewhere in our heads.

That's not all bad. Their presence, for many people, is comforting and warm. I can feel my mother with me, often, when I am in the kitchen or when I am trying on clothes in a store. And when I garden, my father's presence is indefinably there, reassuring, calm, happy. These things give me pleasure.

Two of my own children, now grown up and gone from home, tell me the smell of burnt coffee has a peculiar warmth for them. They are coming in from school, the coffee pot has burnt dry, the kitchen is filled with smoke; that means Mom's story must be rolling and all is well with the world.

Each of us needs to talk firmly to these ghosts. Meshing several sets of values is not easy. Accommodation, communication—and perhaps distance from families of origin that are reluctant to let go—are all sometimes necessary as we go about creating a new family (even if it's a family of one) that has its own unique values, that is not a replica of the old ones that gave it birth. But that is one of the many tasks of adulthood.

inances

Because most of us attach a lot of unresolved energy to money and finances, they can be extremely disruptive in a relationship. One partner, for example, may come from a family which is fairly relaxed about money; the priorities are to have a good time and worry about retirement when it comes along. The other partner believes in saving like mad and has to be dragged on vacation.

Even if these extremes are cushioned, even if both partners agree on how to spend and save money, money matters can still create problems. One woman whose marriage had just collapsed said to me gently after we had taken out our first-ever mortgage (and were still shaking): "Don't do what we did. We worked so hard to pay it off in a hurry we forgot about each other."

So talk. And talk and talk. Money, sex and children are all areas where we need to communicate well.

Guilt

In one way or another, guilt affects most relationships at some time. A good job will be passed by because one party in the relationship doesn't want to move; harsh remarks will be made in a moment of anger; a wrong decision will prevail.

Sometimes guilt isn't necessary at all. We confuse it with self-doubt.

And guilt is not a productive emotion. Repentance is better. Repentance means moving past guilt by acknowledging it, apologizing, doing what is possible to provide restoration, and then leaving it behind.

Of course, sometimes you can't restore things the way they were, especially in relationships. Too much has happened. This is life. It is full of human failure and error. A large dose of self-acceptance is in order, as well as knowing when to let go. It's all right to just say good-bye sometimes.

Then you can mourn. Grief is less damaging than guilt, which is generally corrosive and bitter. Mourning is also something you do together, with someone or several someones. But guilt is a very lonely place.

appiness

People who are happy get along with themselves—and perhaps others—extremely well.

And the Jungians are dead right about this one: happiness doesn't come to those who seek it. It happens by accident. Sometimes you turn around and catch a glimpse of it—in the middle of setting the table, or writing a letter, or at one of those odd times when you observe that you are not, at this very moment, racing for a deadline. (Sometimes even when you're working hard to meet a deadline!) You notice, suddenly, that you are happy.

That's how it works. That's the secret. You don't find happiness. It finds you.

Having said that, there's nothing that says you can't put yourself in the way of happiness by doing the kind of personal inner work that this book talks about.

ntimacy

It's a conundrum. We yearn to be close to another person, to feel as if we were wearing their skin, to have them always understand what we are feeling. That's the way it was when we were babies, and our mothers and ourselves were almost one.

But as soon as we get that close to someone, the hard-earned sense of identity we forged as we grew up becomes threatened, and we flee. It took most of us a long time to wrest ourselves away from that oneness and learn to make our own judgements about the world, different from the judgements of our parents. We constantly strive to see the universe through our own eyes.

Still, at times of stress we look back on that safety with longing. So we have to fight to prevent ourselves from being sucked back into childhood—or so we feel.

We end up doing a kind of dance. We get very close to someone; then we get frightened and back away. That makes our identity more secure, so we move close again. But it again becomes too close for our comfort (people have varying comfort levels with intimacy) and so we pick a fight, or have a severe talk about not-being-ready-for-this relationship or situation. Then we feel strong once more; but the relationship is in pieces once more.

Age or, to be more accurate, maturity helps. As we bounce around the world, and as it bounces us around, we begin to understand what our boundaries are. We find ways to communicate our unease more gently, when someone presses. And our identity feels more solid; it is not quite as scary to let someone get close to us.

SADNESS SHARED IS HALVED

JOY SHARED IS DOUBLED

 **J**oy

Happiness can be solitary. It is a quality independent of others, springing as it does from a clear and present love and acceptance of oneself.

But joy is different. Joy resides in our ability to sustain intimacy with others, to feel their sadness and their joy. We don't get one without the other.

Some people are unable to share in another's joy—although they are often good at sorrow because it is not quite as threatening. A society that emphasizes competition and getting ahead of others, as much as ours does, has difficulty with shared joy.

I once heard Jean Vanier telling his gentle stories about life with the world's forgotten ones. Vanier founded L'Arche, group homes where deeply mentally handicapped people live in community with their friends, himself among them. He seems without ambition, content to spend his life in the company of those who will never command a corporate salary or write a best-seller.

"But shouldn't we work hard, to try to be successful?" a young student asked him. "Because, if we don't, we'll be left behind."

"Yes," answered Vanier, with delight. "Yes, that's it! We will be left behind. We will sing and dance and have a marvellous time, there, together, at the end of the line!"

Which gives us another clue about joy. Happiness comes from within. Satisfaction comes from doing one's best and discovering excellence. But joy comes from a life lived in relationship with others. We need all three in our lives.

itchen

Eating together is a powerful component in relationships. Who cooks for whom, who does the grocery shopping, and who gets served by whom, even what is served and where, are all crucial ways of defining power structures in the home. You might want to look at it in your own life. You might even want to make some changes.

ove

There are different kinds of love. You knew that already.

There's the kind of love you feel when you have just discovered someone perfect. The world is illuminated and warmed somehow from within, and logic—even for the most binary mind—is temporarily dismissed.

This kind of love passes. If you are very wise and very lucky, infatuation transmutes itself gently into something more realistic. You grow to see the faults of the other, and to accept them without trying to change the other person. It helps if you understand that happiness comes from within yourself, not from the loved one, and it helps if you have the patience to let this love grow to its own, more solid, fruition.

For most of us, this movement is not smooth and easy. The relationship may crumble along the way. Most of us survive such crumblings, albeit with pain.

Advice: Enjoy the heady period of love, with all its projections (See P); but at the same time be aware that it will change and grow. Our dreams of the ways we would like the other to be (he is always so wise, she is always so gentle and self-effacing) may have to be revised. The job of a long-term relationship is not to turn others into whatever we want them to be. It is to love them as they are.

Marriage, by the way, puts a real twister into this. The person you have, until now, loved with considerable intensity and often much illogic, suddenly becomes Husband or Wife. Both are terms around which we have a lot of expectations, founded in our own families of childhood. "Wife" may be someone who bakes cookies; "Husband" may be someone who fixes leaky taps. If the person doesn't measure up to the expectation, the plummet into reality for

both of you can be treacherous.

The other twister, in marriage, is that just at the moment your spouse slides into the cold light of reality, and you discover hitherto unnoted idiosyncrasies—like a tendency to fill the sink with dirty dishes, or to leave the bathtub littered with hair—someone else will appear in the rosy light of first love. Don't assume you are immune. Few are. Marriage ceremonies, and all those parties and presents from the relatives, are designed to make it inconvenient to undo the knot too impulsively.

If you can survive the first few times this happens, without drifting into bed (which complicates things painfully) you will eventually note that these white-hot relationships either turn themselves into comfortable friendships, or vanish. The cold light of reality eventually gets turned on them too, and we see them as they really are—not the Goddess herself, or a Knight in shining armour. Just another human being.

Meantime, repeat the mantra of love: "My job is not to turn others into what I want them to be. It is to love them as they are."

Masks or personae

One of the ways we avoid intimacy—and therefore, relationships of depth—is by assuming disguises which may or may not reflect the person within.

The mask of a profession, for example, is one of the most convenient. At parties (where, as an introverted type, I am often at a loss) I sometimes find myself interviewing people. Threatened by the need to somehow communicate with all these people, I don the mask of the journalist. I can pass an evening busily getting inside peoples' heads, never letting anyone inside my own. Since there's not much shared on my part, there's not much joy in this (although it is interesting, and often productive later, if I'm looking for contacts for a story). Not much relaxation either, which is what I have heard parties are supposed to be about.

This is not entirely a bad tendency. We all need masks. Doctors, couldn't function if they had to greet patients, whom they must literally see naked, without the barrier of the profession between them. Teachers have to accept the authority of their profession, if they are to command attention. Therapists must wear the appropriate mask, so their clients can trust them to work from an authoritative study of human behaviour as well as their own intuition.

There are other masks we can assume. Mother (a mask that some of us wear in all kinds of relationships) or Father or omnipotent and self-sacrificing Friend. But we also need to be aware that these are simply garments we put on to do the task at hand; underneath there is still a human being with feelings and fears. If we love another person, and wish to continue a relationship with them, there have to be moments when those vulnerabilities show. Without those moments, there may be companionship and learning, but no joy.

Numinous

Numinous is not a word in great favor; our times prefer the scientific and technological. The second dictionary I consulted (the first didn't even recognize the word) defines it as " the combined feeling of attraction and awe characteristic of a sense of communion with God."

What does that have to do with our relationships with others? Not much, maybe. On the other hand, it's a handy term to describe the indescribable moments in human relationships too: the moment a child is born; the first time you and another grow something together, a bunch of impatiens or geraniums; or times when you go for a long walk and feel a great peace just from being together.

Some would argue that such moments are spiritual. Some would argue, too, that such moments point to the kind of relationship God yearns to have with us, the kind of relationship for which we were created. And that God takes pleasure in our joy.

Ommmmmm...

Some people do yoga or meditate. Some pray. Some (those who can afford it) go to an analyst; some—often in crisis, so they are forced to it—go to a therapist. Some do all of the above, although not always concurrently. Some chant "om" at odd moments during the day. It lifts them out of themselves.

Personality types

There are many ways to define the similarities and differences between people. There's Myers-Briggs, a system developed by two Jungians that identifies sixteen distinct patterns by which people approach the world. (When I call myself an "intuitive feeler," I'm using Myers-Briggs language.) There's the Enneagram, an ancient Sufi system recently resurrected mainly within the Roman Catholic church.

Jungians also like to talk about particular archetypes that seem to have more power in one person than another, helping to define their personality.

If you go back to "A" in this book, you will see that we have opted to define "aerobics" and "abandonment" rather than "archetype." That's because archetype is so hard to define. But if you've got this far in this book, you're probably gracious enough to put up with a stab at it.

An archetype is a kind of powerful framework we carry around inside, to which we can fasten images and feelings—a sort of coat-rack for emotions and motivations, a place where they are collected into a recognizable form. Some archetypes are named for myths and images, some after the old gods and goddesses. Since each of us tends to favor (or be favored by) certain archetypes over others, it becomes possible to recognize which old gods and myths are at play in us. These give a shape to our personality, and a way of naming it.

An example: the other day I went to the linen cupboard to look for some sheets. We had unexpected company and I needed to make up the spare beds. But every sheet I pulled out was covered with spray paint. "WELCOME HOME,

Davey-O!" said the first one. "WELCOME HOME, Andy!" was sprayed on the second. And so on. Whenever our now-grown children had travelled away from home, my husband had turned our biggest sheets, one after another, into signs to hang on the garage door when they came back.

I collapsed into laughter, pawing ineffectively through the cupboard trying to find something to put on the guests' beds. Jung would say this extravagance on my husband's part springs from the archetype of the *puer*—the eternal youth

You can recognize other archetypes at play in people if you watch. I myself like to play Wise Philosopher, when I have the chance.

Projection

This is a useful term to describe our very human tendency to "project" certain traits outwards onto other people. Often, they're traits we possess ourselves. We could see those traits clearly that way, if we knew to look. But usually, we just lose sight of the fact that they are part of us.

It's particularly important in a relationship with someone of the opposite sex to know what projection is about. It's the reason we fall in love with people: we project all sorts of marvellous traits onto them that we would like them, need them, to have. It's also the reason we develop indefinable hatreds for others. We project our own angers and frustrations outwards as well.

So our initial starry-eyed romance with someone, for example, is usually based on projection. This is not a bad thing. It's the stuff of legend and heart-stopping drama. The work, when you are into a relationship for the long haul, comes in dropping the projections and still loving the other, this time for what they *really* are.

The best advice for times in the grip of an unfamiliar and passionate love or passionate hatred may be that given to anyone who finds themselves in strange territory: Don't panic. Remember to breathe. Sit down and think. Try to get to some kind of high ground where you can look around and see the overall picture. Clarity of vision will eventually return; the angel or devil you have discovered will reappear as an ordinary human being.

In the meantime—if it's a positive projection—go ahead and enjoy the way the world shimmers.

Question

Here's the most -asked question in human relationships: do you really love me? Understanding the nature of projection is the beginning of an answer to that question. Really loving someone is when the image placed on them by your projections falls away, and you see their strange quirks and the way they tell the same joke fifty times before it's worn out and the horrible way they screw up the toothpaste tube… and you still love them.

Really loving someone is still bothering to make them laugh.

Really loving someone is trusting that you yourself are loveable and capable of love.

elaxation

Some people find the whole business of actually having to relate to others unbearably tense. If you're one of those people, we hope reading books like this at least helps relax your mind about it.

On the other hand, if you relax your body, your mind generally follows. So take a bath. Listen to a soothing tape. And above all, remember to breathe. Deeply, evenly, freely...

ex

We liked this cartoon, and the only way we could think of to use it was to include this heading. But we aren't going to presume to give advice. Except that if you cherish your significant relationship in other ways, this aspect of your relationship will probably flourish too.

**S**oul

It's helpful, in relationships, to know that we are creatures with souls—sometimes called our "higher self" or "cosmic self." This makes us God's companions. We believe that God loves us unconditionally, and accompanies us, and shows God's face to us in small acts of human kindness. That belief may help sustain us at a patchy time in other relationships.

eenagers

Their wonderful, clear-eyed vision of the world can make you doubt your own sanity, desirability, or capacity to hang onto *any* relationships. They see your warts so clearly, and they need them. That crystalline understanding of just where you went wrong in your life is, for many of them, the way they can begin to shape their own personalities differently.

Whisper to yourself that real learning comes from standing on the shoulders of giants; those who have gone before offer wisdom to those who follow, so they can build on it. That's what teenagers are doing. You are the giant, and they are trying to take off from your shoulders into some pinnacle of wisdom you **almost** reached.

It's just that the taking-off can be a little painful sometimes.

Therapy

There's a difference between curing and healing. There are a lot of things from which we cannot be **cured**. Ancient scars will always remain, forgiveness is hard. The notion that our dark sides could ever be taken away from us is both laughable and dangerous. It's wise to remember that racism and rage sit like banked fires within us all.

But we can be **healed**. We can come to know some of the contents of our unconscious, and live graciously with them. That's healing. Some people can find healing in a strong and welcoming faith community. Some people can do it themselves with work and discipline and study and prayer. And sometimes a good spiritual director, or therapist, or friend, can help move along.

ransference

Transference is a special form of projection found in counselling situations. It describes how—without knowing we are doing it—we take material from our childhood, memories, images, impressions tucked away in our unconscious from when we were little, and transfer them onto the helping person. We might transfer all our feelings for our father or mother onto this figure who seems powerful enough to carry them. Ministers, doctors, therapists, sometimes classroom teachers are often the objects of this kind of activity.

As adults, we can be healed of a lot of childhood hurts while in the grip of transference. It's kind of a second run at learning the rules of life. However, it's also a period when we are, necessarily, very vulnerable. If the recipient of all these feelings is someone of the opposite sex, the relationship can create a powerful passion. If she or he is unaware or untrained or unsupported by others, then counter-transference (an equal amount of passion for the helpee) may ensue.

That's why its good to understand what the term means, and very good not to trust your psychological health to the unscrupulous or unskilled.

UNCONSCIOUS   COLLECTIVE UNCONSCIOUS

nconscious

We **think** we know what we are doing, as we relate to other people. The fact is, we usually don't. As the cartoon on page 98 implies, our interactions with our children, mates and friends are shaped profoundly by our pasts, our memories and beliefs and stereotypes and all the unconscious, unknown-to-us ways we see the world.

It's extremely helpful to know this. Every once in a while—through dreams, through an unusually brave and candid friend, through an insight at church or in a recovery group—we get a sideways glimpse of our own unconscious and what/who rests there. If there's an ambitious woman within, you can talk to her, and see where she is going. If there is a controlling parent affecting you and your relationship with your own child or partner, you may be able to negotiate it into a truce. If there is a terribly hungry, needy child that gets you into frequent painful romances, you may be able love her or him into being a little more self-sufficient.

There are further complications. Jung came up with the notion of the collective unconscious, the idea that we are mysteriously connected to others in this realm. So we have people who dream large dreams that draw on the collective unconscious of a whole nation or culture. Wise figures like Jesus or Moses or Gandhi were able to touch the yearnings of their people at a very deep level. We also have not-so-wise people who are able to draw only darkness out of our shared unconscious.

That's why it's good to know about our unconscious, and be wary of being manipulated by some of the figures within it.

Validation

There's nothing quite like you-and-me-against-the-universe to strengthen a relationship. In its darkest aspect, this is how cults work. They offer its members validation—we, and we only, are doing/thinking the right thing—against a hostile society.

But in more ordinary relationships, validation is a wonderful source of strength. You can see it most clearly in couples who share some of the same personality characteristics, ones that are not especially valued by the world. But the couple understand each other. There is a lovely scene in the film *Untamed Heart* where the heroine, who has fallen in love with an outsider, someone who doesn't fit anyone's notions of what is attractive, declares to her friend, "He doesn't make sense. And I don't make sense. But together, the two of us, we make sense."

So (if you look back to the section on personality types) you have two intuitives getting toegther, two artists, two dreamers helping each other see that the way they see the world is legitimate. That's validation. It's wonderful.

arrior

This is a useful image to carry around inside ourselves. Although men who go out in the woods and drum in search of their inner warrior have been a favorite joke in the popular press, their search is a valid one. Men and women both need spiritual courage. Life is hard. It's seldom fair. And the darknesses we carry within us are very daunting.

Once, a long time ago, I was heading off on an assignment about which I was afraid. I can't remember where it was, but it was some place scary enough that I was worried I wouldn't do a good job. My hands would shake, my pictures would be blurred, I wouldn't ask the right questions, all that money would have been spent to get me to this faraway place for nothing.

And then I had a dream. A tough, grizzled old reporter came, read me a story, and insisted I read one to him. Then he parked himself in my living room and said he would be staying for awhile.

When I woke up, I felt a lot better. My warrior had arrived. He stayed with me all through that assignment. My hands didn't shake and my photos were fine, and I told the story, just as he had requested.

Never dismiss an archetype. Especially not the warrior. We need heart if we are going to tackle life and the relationships it offers us. You may remember the story of Jacob, who struggled all night with a shadowy figure—an angel perhaps, or God, or his own shadow side. As with many human interactions, Jacob neither wins nor loses. He simply prevails, survives, endures and is wounded, changed forever. For his courage, the angel leaves him with a blessing.

That's the blessing of the warrior. It's one we all can use.

ork

We could write all kinds of scholarly things about work. How for some it becomes an addiction. How many of us get our identity from our work; at a social gathering, the question we're most likely to ask a total stranger is, "So what do you do?"

But we won't. We just like this cartoon.

in Yang

Yin Yang comes to us from China. It's a way of seeing, a way in which everything exists in relation to something else. Its central theme is contrast: vertical with horizontal, soft with hard, passive with active, contracting with expanding, masculine with feminine...

It's an esoteric concept, but it's a good way of allowing ourselves to be different from one another.

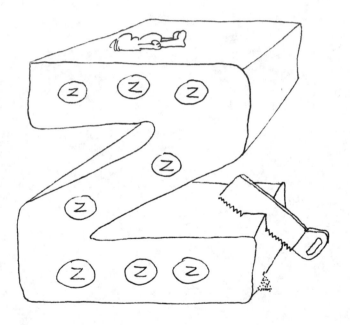

**ZZZ**

The end of the book. We hope we haven't put you to sleep.

Time for a test. Can you live beyond projections, learn to communicate, enjoy the reality of your loved one...?

Postscript

When we wrote this book, we pictured—for some reason—someone rushing through an airport, picking up this book in the bookstore just before boarding, and reading it all through the flight. It should take from Vancouver to Toronto. Or vice versa. Depending on how fast you read, you could get off at your destination with a new understanding of the way the human heart works.

But that wasn't quite the right picture. Understanding the human heart takes a little longer than that. And when we really thought it through, we realized that this book isn't just for air travelers or people who ride on the subway, or people having trouble with the ones they love. It is for anyone who would like a touch of laughter with their everyday human relationships, and a small glimmer of understanding with the confusion of daily life.

We'll be happy if it has provided that. And if chuckling over these drawings, or meditating on some of these ideas for a few minutes (say, in the dentist's office, while waiting for your filling to harden), makes one of your interactions with someone else just a little deeper, then we will be even happier.

—Donna Sinclair
—Allan Hirsh

By Donna Sinclair and Yvonne Stewart

Christian Parenting
Raising children in the real world

Being a parent can be one of the most difficult and challenging jobs today. Being Christian makes the job no easier. *Christian Parenting* helps parents in a competitive, me-first society. This book offers the honesty and support that parents need.

5.5 " x 8.5", 124 pages, softcover, Wood Lake Books
919-091 • **$ 12.95**

Available from:
Wood Lake Books, PO Box 700, Winfield, BC V0H 2C0
Order line: toll-free **1-800-663-2775**

Also by Donna Sinclair

Worth Remembering

A guide to writing your autobiography.

Donna Sinclair takes you step-by-step through the how's and why's of writing your own story. Ordinary people should write their memoirs, too.

5.5" x 8.5", 112 pages, softcover, Wood Lake Books
919-094 • **$ 9.95**

Available from:
Wood Lake Books, PO Box 700, Winfield, BC V0H 2C0
Order line: toll-free **1-800-663-2775**

Madam, I'm Adam
and other takes
on the Old Testament

By Philip Street

These biblical comic strips retell familiar stories which are part of the overall story. Many vignettes are set in modern terms, prompting the reader to laugh initially and reflect more deeply later.

5.5" x 8.5", 112 pages, softcover, Wood Lake Books
929-074 • **$ 7.95**